C000182847

LONDON BUSES IN COLOUR: 1970s

Kevin McCormack

Only on a Sunday

Front cover: One-person operation of RT Route 71 is illustrated by RF528 picking up at the Dysart Arms at Petersham. This stop was noteworthy for retaining the old-style separate bus and coach flags. *Mike Pope*

Imposter

Back cover: With no 'On-hire' sticker in the windscreen, LT appears to have sneaked a journey on LCBS Route 418. This view shows MB72 in Church Road, Bookham, on 1 June 1975. *Michael Furnell*

Kingston Trio

Title page: LT and LCBS are represented on 20 May 1978 by Sutton's DMS260 and Leatherhead's RMC1464 and SM111. *Geoff Rixon*

Earache

Left: The provision of piped music and foreign language advertising failed to lure sufficient passengers on to the sponsored Shoplinker services which lasted for under six months in 1979. RM2154, seen here at Marble Arch, was one of 16 Stockwell-based RMs to receive the striking red and yellow livery. *John May*

Three-Year Itch

Right: The ECW-bodied Bristol VRT was popular with other NBC companies but not so with LCBS which bought 15 in 1977 and then sold them in 1980. Grays garage received the whole class and this view depicts BT7 at Romford. *John May*

First published 1999

ISBN 0 7110 2701 3

All rights reserved. No part of this book may be reproduced or transmitted in any form or by any means, electronic or mechanical, including photocopying, recording or by any information storage and retrieval system, without permission from the Publisher in writing.

© Kevin McCormack 1999

Published by Ian Allan Publishing

an imprint of Ian Allan Publishing Ltd, Terminal House, Shepperton, Surrey TW17 8AS.

Printed by Ian Allan Printing Ltd, Riverdene Business Park, Hersham, Surrey KT12 4RG.

Code: 9909/C

Introduction

Those of us who were around in the 1970s will all have our different recollections of that period: decimalisation, Glam Rock, galloping inflation, the three-day week, the 'winter of discontent' and, particularly for Londoners like myself, broken down buses.

The decade opened with the biggest upheaval, until then, that London Transport (LT) had experienced since its creation in 1933. LT's country bus and Green Line coach services were transferred on 1 January 1970 to a newly-formed subsidiary of the National Bus Company (NBC) called London Country Bus Services (LCBS). This was a direct consequence of the transfer of LT to the now defunct Greater London Council which would only be responsible for controlling services in its own area, ie the London boroughs. Fortunately, the GLC boundary roughly coincided with the division between Central Area (red) and Country Area (green) buses and so structuring the split was relatively simple.

LCBS set out to create its own identity and to shake off its LT ancestry. Out went the famous bull's-eye motif wherever possible, although it survived on bus stops for most of the decade. In came a new logo which actually resembled a winged bull's-eye and came to be nicknamed the 'flying polo' (or, less politely, the 'flying bedpan'!) Vehicle liveries were brightened up a little, with the universal application of yellow to replace the old cream relief (a process started by LT) and the introduction of a slightly lighter shade of green. But, alas, LCBS's attempts at individuality did not fit the NBC's corporate image and in 1972 NBC imposed its own logo and livery (all-over leaf green, sometimes with white relief).

LT and LCBS shared a common goal of updating their ageing fleets and achieving 100% one-person operation (OPO) as quickly as possible in the decade, thereby eradicating the late 1940s/early 1950s RT and RF classes, and then the Routemaster (RM). Unfortunately for the operators, the replacement vehicles, particularly the large fleets of Merlins, Swifts and Fleetlines (DMSs), and also some of the Green Line coaches, proved to be unreliable and the position was exacerbated by a chronic shortage of spares for many classes, including the RM. To the delight of enthusiasts, the RTs and RFs soldiered on until 1979 and the green Routemasters (RMCs, RCLs and RMLs) just reached 1980. Only then did LCBS meet its OPO objective, something which in the end LT never did. Indeed, by the close of the 1970s, LT had performed an amazing U-turn by purchasing every secondhand Routemaster it could lay its hands on.

For much of the decade, both LT and LCBS were reduced to buying or hiring vehicles from other operators as they struggled to keep their services going. However, there was light appearing at the end of the tunnel. The Leyland Nationals brought improved standards of reliability, followed later by the introduction by LT of two new double-deck types: the Leyland Titan (T class) and the MCW Metrobus (M class) which are still operating in London today, along with a shrunken fleet of rejuvenated Routemasters.

Although we were not to know at the time, the 1970s marked a watershed: the changes which followed in the 1980s and 1990s, arising from route tendering and the break-up of LT and LCBS, have altered the London bus scene beyond all recognition. The 1970s represent a bygone age and I hope readers will enjoy reliving the atmosphere of those days through the pages of this book. I have tried to provide a wide geographical spread and to concentrate on the classes which are most associated with that era.

Finally, may I thank all the photographers who have generously provided their precious material: Michael Furnell, Steve Fennell, John May, Geoff Rixon, Mike Pope, the late Mike Harries, Dave Brown, Roy Hobbs, Peter Plummer and Dave Edwards.

Kevin R. McCormack
Ashtead, Surrey
July 1999

Here Today, Gone Tomorrow

Left: RT3871 mixes with Routemasters and Daimler Fleetlines at Catford garage on 24 August 1978. The next day would see the end of RT operation on Route 94 and the isolation of the last RTs to Barking's 62 and 87 services. *Michael Furnell*

Desperate Measures

Above: In October 1977, Dartford garage was forced to press 25-year-old unmodernised RF221 into Green Line service to cover vehicle shortages. This old warhorse later became the penultimate LCBS RF, surviving for another 12 months on passenger duties. *Steve Fennell*

WOOLWICH
SOYA WANNA COOKIN OIL?
Percy Dalton's
PURE SOYA OIL
Go wherever you want with a Red Bus Rover Ticket.
Oxford Circus
Charing + Elephant
New + Woolwich
53
OXFORD CIRCUS
Go wherever you want with a Red Bus Rover Ticket.
TELEPHONE
DM 937
SMU937N
53
CAMDEN TOWN
OUC 121R
LEFT TURN

Bad Omen

Left: This end-of-the-decade shot at Woolwich depicts crew-operated Fleetline DM937, deputising for a Metropolitan (MD), illustrated here by MD121. By September 1980, a start was made on permanently replacing MDs on Route 53. *Steve Fennell*

Unwelcome Legacy

Below: LCBS had 138 AEC Swifts foisted upon it, the order having been placed by LT prior to the split. SM491 climbs Gravel Hill, Bexleyheath, on 13 May 1979; the A2 Rochester Way curves away into the distance. *Michael Furnell*

Coastal Connections

Prestige was restored to Green Line services with the arrival of the RB (Reliance Blackpool) and RS (Reliance Scarborough) coaches, these seaside resorts being the locations of the Duple and Plaxton factories which produced the bodies for these vehicles. RB24 and RB46 meet on Eccleston Bridge, Victoria, in 1978. *Steve Fennell*

To Bookham in Style

RN9, seen at Surbiton on 16 July 1978, brings a touch of luxury to a route previously operated by Swifts. The RNs were Plaxton-bodied AEC Reliances acquired by LCBS from Barton Transport of Nottingham in 1977. *Geoff Rixon*

Well Worth Keeping

LT was pleased with the Leyland National type which was originally purchased as a stopgap replacement for the Swifts. Leaving Heathrow bus station on 12 March 1978 is LS31, one of 51 Phase 2 Nationals (LS7-57) which were originally destined for Venezuela. *Geoff Rixon*

Red Triangle

Despite the colour on the radiator, the 68 standard-length Routemaster coaches were always green (until resold to LT). Here, RMC1483 heads south down Barn End Lane, Wilmington, on 27 August 1979, while working one of the last LCBS Routemaster routes. *Michael Furnell*

Country Life

Another unwanted LT Merlin, MB119, experiences the charms of Brockham on 22 August 1974 while on hire to LCBS. *Michael Furnell*

Fading Supremacy

Above: LT started the decade with 2,775 RTs in passenger service, just making this the largest single class. By the beginning of 1977, the number had dwindled to around 500, including Palmers Green's RT679, which was photographed in Hampden Way, near Arnos Grove, on 3 September 1977. *Peter Plummer*

Keeping up Appearances

Right: Onslow Street bus station, Guildford, is the setting for RF120, one of 175 RFs modernised in 1966/7 in order to update the Green Line image. This involved the fitting of twin headlamps, a single-piece driver's windscreen, fluorescent interior lighting and a wide central relief band edged with aluminium strips. *Mike Pope*

DORKING STATION
425 CHILWORTH GOMSHALL
LONDON COUNTRY
PAY AS YOU ENTER PLEASE
LYF 471
Cafe
U S E C A Rs

You could drive this bus
Apply for details at any London Country garage
DRIVERS needed NOW!
LONDON COUNTRY
Broxbourne
Cheshunt Waltham X
310
ENFIELD
Take off anywhere, anyday, with
GOLDEN ROVER
AN5 HG 5
JPL 105K

Last Year's Colour

Left: Leyland Atlantean AN5, representing LCBS's OPO replacement for the RTs and Routemasters, was the company's answer to LT's silver RMs. Repainted to commemorate HM The Queen's Silver Jubilee in 1977, the vehicle still looked smart when photographed on 6 May 1978 in Enfield. *Geoff Rixon*

First of the Many

Above: A total of 413 AEC Regal IV buses and coaches came over to LCBS in 1970 including RF26, seen here at Dorking in October 1974. This, the first production Green Line RF coach, dating from 1951, was one of those modernised in 1966/7. This variation of NBC livery seems to suit the vehicle. *Mike Harries*

On the Open Road

Below: RT1015 approaches Ongar on 24 March 1976 during the last week of RT operation on Harlow's Route 339. Five days later, blue and white Leyland half-cab double-deckers arrived, borrowed from Southend Transport following use by LT. *Michael Furnell*

RF Operating Day

Right: LT started the decade with 233 RFs which, combined with LCBS's fleet, meant that only 54 members of the 700-strong class had been withdrawn. This view of Norbiton's RF513 at Cobham dates from 26 September 1974. RFs can, of course, still be seen in this area, courtesy of the nearby Bus Museum. *Michael Furnell*

KINGSTON
215 Street Cobham
Esher
ANTHONY
BERNARD
PAY AS YOU ENTER
PLEASE
MXX 490
PAY AS YOU ENTER PLEASE
BUS STOP
215

The People's Choice

Left: LN3, the third of 543 LCBS Leyland Nationals, is overtaken by MS3 from the meagre class of seven Metro-Scanias. Both vehicles carry the striking Stevenage Superbus livery, selected by the public in preference to green and yellow and first introduced on 31 July 1971. *John May*

High Hopes

Right: Between December 1975 and February 1977, LT took delivery of 164 Metropolitan (MD) double-deckers in a vain attempt to find a superior vehicle to the Daimler Fleetline. The MDs were an amalgamation of Metro-Cammell Weymann bodies and Scania-Vabis running units from Sweden and proved to be more powerful and less noisy than the DMS. However, problems with corrosion and spare parts consigned the class to an early grave and the last one ran on 24 June 1983 (MD127). In the summer of 1979, while still crew-operated, MD64 approaches Marble Arch. *John May*

Paddington Victoria
Camberwell New +
Lewisham Downham
36B
WEST KILBURN
Phone
836 3456
GAS GETS ON WITH IT...
...working for a better Britain.
36B
GROVE PARK
KJD 264P

Smile Please!

The 21-strong SMA class of AEC Swift coaches entered service in 1972 on Green Line duty, having originally been ordered by South Wales Transport. The panoramic windows in the Scottish-built Alexander bodies were popular with passengers but the fleet suffered, like so many other types, from mechanical problems and most were withdrawn in 1978. SMA4 finished its days on mundane bus work in the Dartford/Gravesend area and the fact that anyone should want to photograph the vehicle is clearly puzzling the locals. *John May*

Ugly Duckling

BS2 was one of 17 short and ungainly looking ECW-bodied Bristols purchased in 1975/6. 24ft long and seating 26 passengers, these vehicles had manual transmission and the first six were allocated to Route C11 (Willesden Green to Archway Station), replacing Ford Transit (FS class) minibuses. The BS type was withdrawn by July 1981. *John May*

No TLC

The third largest class to operate in the 1970s, exceeded only by the RTs and Routemasters, was the Daimler Fleetline (DM/DMS class), which totalled 2,646 units. This view of DMS2089 at Romford illustrates the lack of care bestowed on these vehicles, in contrast with the RM behind. *John May*

Ewell Road
Tolworth
Stoneleigh
Ewell Epsom
406
REDHILL STN
POLO
Advertisemint.
LH 2
RT 4117
LUC 466

Time Warp

Left: A total of 484 RTs was transferred from LT on 1 January 1970 but RT4117 seems to have been in hiding because 3½ years of LCBS ownership has had little impact on its appearance. Although the 'flying polo' has arrived (to accompany the poster!), this presentable vehicle carries gold lettering, cream central relief band and an LT radiator badge. The location is Reigate garage. *Roy Hobbs*

Class Distinction

Above: AEC, Leyland and Bristol combine to produce an impressive array of LT vehicles outside the old Staines West railway station in Wraysbury Road. From left to right are LS48, RM1281, RF521 and BL50. *Mike Pope*

Joint Venture

Below: The Leyland National was a collaboration between British Leyland and NBC, which probably accounted for LCBS's buying so many. LNC33, standing opposite Romford garage in February 1973, was an example of the original long coach version. *Steve Fennell*

Going East

Right: Leyland Atlantean XA19 displays the short-lived open LT roundel in this view at Peckham Rye in January 1973. Later that year, after only eight years service, the entire class of 50 was sold to Hong Kong. *Steve Fennell*

red bus rovers
P3
PECKHAM &
NUNHEAD
CIRCULAR
VIA NUNHEAD LANE
red bus rovers
VISITOR'S LONDON
PAY AS YOU ENTER
Exact fare, please
ADULT FARE
4p
CUV 19C
XA19
PAY AS YOU ENTER
Exact fare, please

Sinking Feeling

Left: Both LT and LCBS experimented with Ford Transit minibuses on 'stop anywhere' services. Parked at Golders Green station in summer 1977, FS21 displays its 16-seat Strachans bodywork and low driving position. *Steve Fennell*

Not Worth the Effort

Below left: Pulling out of Slough bus station in September 1978 is MBS4, the last of the 15 original Strachans-bodied AEC Merlins to remain in service. This bus started life on the inaugural Red Arrow Route 500 in April 1966, and was the subject of a pilot overhaul at Aldenham Works in 1972. As a result, LT decided to cut its losses and withdraw the entire Merlin class. LCBS snapped up MBS4 and exchanged it with MBS15, the only early Merlin the company had inherited from LT. *Steve Fennell*

Optical Illusion

Right: This rural scene is actually beside a bus garage (Chelsham). RF684, the last of its class to remain in Lincoln Green, is standing in the forecourt while RCL2243 has just arrived from Warlingham Park Hospital. The RCL class consisted of 43 long Routemaster coaches built in 1965 for Green Line service and relegated to bus work in the 1970s. *Mike Pope*

RF684
Super Coach EXPRESS
LONDON-EDINBURGH/GLASGOW ONLY £7
DAY and NIGHT SERVICES ALL YEAR!
403
WEST CROYDON
LONDON COUNTRY
RCL 2243
CUV 243C

Smoke Signal

Above: SNB227 indicates right while its contemporary pollutes the atmosphere at Chadwell St Mary in July 1979. These Leyland Nationals represent the smaller bus version which, at 10.3m, was a metre shorter than the first batches. Vehicles after SNB375 were fitted with a new heating system which eliminated the need for the distinctive roof pod. *Steve Fennell*

Wheels of Fortune

Right: The 1970s marked the heyday of all-over advertising on London buses, and at various times over nearly seven years 26 LT Routemasters carried some very colourful liveries. At Mitcham Common, RM686 offers the prospects of what were then very large winnings. *Geoff Rixon Collection*

VERNONS
THE BEST
88
Shepherds Bush
Oxford Cir. Charing +
Clapham Mitcham
ACTON GREEN
BET IN POOLS
VERNONS
THE BEST BET IN POOLS
The route to a fortune of
£225,000
VERNONS
WLT 686

Too Close for Comfort

GS13, now the doyen of the Surrey Leisure Bus services, looks rather vulnerable standing alongside a disaster area (RM50) at Aldenham Works in September 1973. Eighteen members of the original class of 84 Guy Specials were transferred to LCBS and the last two remained in service until March 1972. A few were retained by LT as staff buses including GS13 which was based at Abbey Wood. *Mike Harries*

Another Pile of Bricks

Amersham garage, like so many others, has been demolished but, ironically, the original Amersham & District building in the background still survives. AEC Swift SM476 waits to depart for Berkhamsted on 5 August 1976.
Michael Furnell

Get fresh with GUERNSEY TOMS
430
Woodhatch
Redhill General Hospital
REIGATE GARAGE
NEW BARGAINS
GREEN LINE
LONDON COUNTRY
RCL 2259
CUV 259C

Crew Cut

Left: Route 430 was the first country service to have its RTs displaced by Autofare-equipped Merlins back in November 1968. However, for a time a single conductor-operated journey ran in the late afternoon and RCL2259 is seen fulfilling this duty in Sandcross Lane, Reigate, in September 1973. *Roy Hobbs*

No Aerials or Dishes

Below: In a setting more reminiscent of the 1950s, smart-looking RT3243, devoid of a via blind, passes the neat rows of council houses in Heathway, Dagenham, on 24 March 1976. North Street, Romford's Route 139 succumbed to OPO DMS vehicles on 23 July 1977. *Michael Furnell*

Still Standing

Above: LT's 700 AEC Swifts of the SM/SMD/SMS class entered service between November 1969 and February 1972. This shot depicts Marshall-bodied 'standee' SMS172 on 3 March 1976 at Swanley, one of the few ex-LCBS garages to survive today and still be used for its original purpose (by Metrobus). *Michael Furnell*

Drawing a Blank

Right: Surplus British European Airways Routemasters were purchased by LT and pressed into service on Romford's Route 175 where RMA4 (formerly BEA No 29) is seen in March 1976. LT's decision not to install blind boxes added to the general unpopularity of these front-entrance vehicles and they were soon relegated to non-public use. *Dave Brown*

BRITISH RAILWAYS
FREQUE
TO LONDON
RED BUS PASS
£7.50
RED BUS PASS
£7.50
RED BUS PASS
175
NORTH ROMFORD
DAGENHAM
175
RMA 4
NMY 629E
YHK 514F
9LN2094

Wise Move

Route 410, once the preserve of the celebrated 'Godstone STLs', was endowed with LCBS's first new double-deckers in February 1972. These were 11 Leyland-engined Daimler Fleetlines with Northern Counties bodywork, a diverted order from Western Welsh. The decision to buy so few Fleetlines proved sensible in the light of LT's experiences with its huge fleet. *John May*

Shades of Glory

Contrasting with AF2's new mid-green livery is RC4's ageing Lincoln Green with pale green relief, a legacy from the 1960s. Seen here at Aldgate, RC4 was one of the 14 RC class AEC Reliances with 49-seat Willowbrook bodies introduced in 1965 for Green Line services. *John May*

Pratts Bottom

This distinctively named place near Sevenoaks provides an opportunity to see a further colour scheme, this time NBC leaf green as carried by RP60. The RPs were the first Green Line coaches ordered by LCBS but, yet again, they proved unreliable. The last example (RP25) ran in LCBS service on 18 February 1984. This photograph was taken on 23 June 1976, a month before the pursuing vehicle, RF129, was withdrawn. *Michael Furnell*

Embellished

Below: The unpainted aluminium strips enhance this smart-looking standee Merlin, MBS295, operating in LCBS's northwestern extremities at Tring in early 1973. The Merlin's excessive length (36ft, compared with 33ft 5in for a Swift) seemed to create less of a problem for LCBS than for LT. *Steve Fennell*

On Test

Right: The first of 1,131 Leyland Titans purchased by LT between 1978 and 1984 emerges from Hornchurch garage in October 1978 for a proving trip on Route 246. The initial 250 vehicles followed the old LT tradition of being built at the AEC works and at Park Royal body works. *John May*

LONDON TRANSPOR
HORNCHURCH
PRIVATE
Multi-Ride tickets save you time
Multi-Ride tickets save you money
PLEASE PAY AS YOU ENTER
OJD142R
TITAN
No. 1
MULTI-RIDE
A New Leyland Titan for London Transport
OUT
PLEASE PAY AS YOU ENTER
LEYLAND TITAN
THX 401S

Take us for all we've got
14
Kings Cross Euston
Piccadilly
Knightsbridge
S. Kensington Fulham
STAMFORD BRIDGE
LONDON TRANSPORT
RT 3257
LLU 616
UNDERGROUND

Battered but Unbowed

Left: RTs enjoyed an Indian summer in 1976 and 1977 when several had to be drafted in to garages with no RT allocations to cover for RM shortages. Usually, the stray RTs were recognisable by their RM blinds and some were incredibly scruffy, like RT3257, seen at Hyde Park Corner on 5 July 1977. *Peter Plummer*

On Borrowed Time

Above: The last roofbox RTs just survived into the 1970s but some were back on the streets again during 1978, this time privately owned ones hired by LT to supplement the depleted training fleet. Heading a procession down Chiswick High Road is RT191 in mock prewar livery. *Author*

Back Home

Below: The eight XF class Daimler Fleetlines spent most of their lives at East Grinstead but XF8 was posted to Stevenage for a time (see page 70). This view was taken near Felbridge on 12 August 1976 when LT bus stop flags still reigned supreme in the LCBS area. *Michael Furnell*

East End Survivor

Right: LCBS withdrew its last AEC Regent low height double-deckers on 31 July 1970 but LT hung on to some red ones until the demise of Dalston's Route 178 on 16 April 1971. RLH58 was still wearing a cream central relief band but with no sign of a radiator badge when it was caught on camera at Clapton on 31 January 1970. *Roy Hobbs*

178 via Carpenters Rd
STRATFORD MARYLAND STATION
Face the future with PEARL assurance
RLH 58
MXX 258

RF Replacement

Below: October 1973 saw the introduction into service by LCBS of the BL class of ECW-bodied Bristol LHs. BL19, in the hands of a properly dressed driver, is operating the Chesham local service 349. This was an amalgamation of the former routes 348A and B, necessitated because the BL's number aperture was too small to take a suffix letter. *John May*

One for the Road

Right: An awkward reversing manoeuvre requiring a second crew member to assist enabled Loughton's RTs to frequent the Blue Boar at Abridge, in Essex, through to 9 April 1976, when Route 167A was withdrawn and the terminus abandoned. This view of RT2268 was taken just over two weeks before the end. *Michael Furnell*

UE BOAR
Chigwell
Buckhurst Hill
Loughton
Rectory Lane
167A
ABRIDGE VIA
Diana Ross
Mahogany
PLAZA 2
More. The new cigarette that's
long, slim and surprisingly mild.
More
FILTER CIGARETTES
50p
RT 2268
LONDON TRANSPORT
KGU 197
MJD 392L

Take a breath of fresh airways.
PAN AM
177
Elephant New +
Greenwich
Woolwich
NEW CROSS GARAGE
VLT 177

Matching Numbers

Left: 8 June 1975 has dawned a beautiful morning as RM177, on Route 177, leaves Abbey Wood garage on the 6.07am service. This is a positioning journey to enable the vehicle, which has operated a night route terminating at Abbey Wood, to return to its own garage. Gold numerals and fleetnames were becoming increasingly rare by this time except on RTs and RFs. *Michael Furnell*

At Clapton Pond

Above right: LT had six Metro-Scania Anglo-Swedish single-deckers and these were allocated to Dalston in August 1973 for the S2 route. Numbered MS1-6, they were noteworthy for having white-painted roofs but ran only until June 1976 when they were replaced by SMS Swifts and then sold. *Steve Fennell*

In Clapton Pond

Right: The MS class had a good turn of speed which the driver of MS4 failed to appreciate on the first day of service (15 August 1973). *Steve Fennell*

GREEN LINE
725 WINDSOR
BROMLEY CROYDON
SUTTON KINGSTON
PAY AS YOU ENTER PLEASE
GREEN LINE
JPF 106K

Visiting the Royals

Left: Brand-new SMA6 passes Hampton Court Palace (behind the photographer) on its way from Gravesend to Windsor Castle in March 1972. *Mike Harries*

Same but Different

Right: In this view dating from July 1971, XA19 prepares to leave the stand at Hackbridge. Although looking similar because they carried the same style of Park Royal bodywork, the XAs were Leyland Atlanteans, whereas the XFs were Daimler Fleetlines. LT's aim was to compare the performance of the two types with each other and with the long Routemaster (RML). No prizes for guessing the overall winner!
Steve Fennell

Buckswood Drive
Gossops Green
Ifield Avenue
CRAWLEY
BUS STATION
NEW
BARGAINS
GREEN LINE
Littlewoods
PAY AS YOU ENTER PLEASE
CY 41 AN71
LONDON COUNTRY
JPL 171K
BUY A NEW
In the Great Segas Autumn Warm-up
classic
405

All Change

Left: Park Royal-bodied Leyland Atlantean AN71 leaves Crawley bus station on the short-lived 479 service. Formerly Southdown Route 79 until taken over by LCBS in 1971, the 479 was succeeded by the C7 in July 1978, whereupon the number moved to Leatherhead to replace the 418. *John May*

Dented Pride

Right: Modernised RF195, seen arriving at Heathrow Airport bus station in June 1971, presents the fast-disappearing, traditional Green Line image: roof-mounted destination boards, smart paintwork, rear wheel discs and no advertisements. Alas, unrepaired front end damage and a non-matching front wheel are evidence that standards are starting to slip. *Mike Harries*

When you need a light... get the name right.
WATER SHORTAGE
SAVE WATER NOW
via
Hemel Hempstead
Town Centre
322
APSLEY MILLS
LONDON COUNTRY
RT 4521
OLD 741

Final Conquest

Left: RTs began their takeover of country area routes in July 1948. Remarkably, this process did not end until 25 years later when, in July 1973, Hemel Hempstead's Route 322 was converted from single-deckers following a reorganisation of services. This view of RT4521 at Apsley dates from the start of RT operation which lasted until May 1975. *Steve Fennell*

Going Spare

Right: Addlestone's vehicle serviceability problems in late 1977 called for desperate measures which included borrowing surplus RCL2249, fitting it with a Swift blind and finding a conductor. The garage's last crew-operated vehicle turns into East Hill from Woking Road, Maybury. *Steve Fennell*

Limited Vision

Below: Merton's newly overhauled DMS53, photographed outside Craven House, Hampton Court on 3 September 1978, demonstrates the lighting arrangements peculiar to the first 167 members of the class. Subsequent vehicles had their headlights placed further apart to improve visibility at night. *Geoff Rixon*

Shining Example

Right: RM695 waits to cross Charing Cross Road near Soho, on its way down Shaftesbury Avenue towards Piccadilly Circus in June 1977. *Geoff Rixon*

19
Highbury Islington
Piccadilly Sloane Sq
Clapham Junction
CLAPHAM JUNCTION
THE CASSANDRA CROSSING
EMPIRE
FROM MAY 26
THE CASSANDRA CROSSING
EMPIRE
FROM MAY 26
RM695
WLT 695

Information Overload

Below: Some garages such as Dunton Green found that RF blinds were too short for displaying via points for all their routes. The solution was to provide restricted information and reduce the aperture of the blind box. RF663 shows the end result in this view at Farnborough High Street on 6 November 1974. *Michael Furnell*

Unexpected Fame

Right: In late 1978/early 1979, the little-known Route 62 was thrust into the limelight as enthusiasts flocked to Barking to witness the end of the 40-year reign of the RT class in passenger service in London. 7 April 1979 marked the last day; some six months earlier RT4126 is seen heading down Whalebone Lane North, near Chadwell Heath. *Author*

Hainault Chadwell Heath
Valence Avenue
Becontree
Upney Lane
62
BARKING
GASCOIGNE ESTATE
62
LUC 475

New Generation

Left: The mainstay of LT's bus fleet in the 1980s and beyond, the rival M and T classes, entered service in late 1978. 1,485 MCWs were built over a 10-year period and this view shows M31, wearing the obsolete white relief around the upper windows, waiting in traffic at Fulwell on 5 June 1979.
Geoff Rixon

Fitter's Nightmare

Below left: The complete antithesis of LT's standardisation policy is evident in this LCBS line-up at Dorking garage in May 1976. With such a variety of vehicles, it is no wonder that the company had trouble keeping its fleet on the road. From left to right are MB103, RF175, RT4495, AN29, SNC162 and BN34.
Mike Harries

RF Substitute

Right: It was ironic that, as everyone scrambled to photograph RFs on their last routes (218 and 219) in the weeks preceding the replacement of these veterans on 31 March 1979 by Leyland Nationals, there seemed to be an increasing number of unofficial BL workings. Here, in the early weeks of 1979, the photographer caught BL91 in Queens Road, between Hersham and Weybridge. *Steve Fennell*

Esher
Hersham
219
WEYBRIDGE STATION
219 WEYBRIDGE STN
PAY AS YOU ENTER
exact fare please
OJD 91R

THE NEW LEYLAND
TITAN
BRITAIN'S No.1
DOUBLE DECKER
Leyland Vehicles
Friern Barnet
Muswell Hill Bdy
Camden Town
134
TOTTENHAM CT RD STN
THE LEYLAND
NATIONAL
BRITAIN'S No.1
SINGLE DECKER
Leyland Vehicles
Leyland Vehicles
Leaders in passenger transport.
134
TOTTENHAM CT RD STN
NO ENTRY
OMNIBUS
DM2646
THX 646 S

Taking a Risk

Left: Until 1979, no Fleetlines were trusted to carry a special livery for fear of prolonged absences off the road, but then British Leyland plucked up the courage to endorse Leyland-engined DM2646. This was the last of the 400 quieter B20 type and the final Fleetline. The crew-operated vehicle joined 12 RMs in being decorated in Shilibeer colours (albeit a simplified livery) to mark 150 years of the London omnibus; it is seen at Friern Barnet in summer 1979. *Mike Pope*

Politically Incorrect

Above: This LT-designed rear-engined Routemaster was the prototype for a fleet that might have brought salvation in the 1970s, had LT not been forced to buy off-the-peg buses instead. FRM1 is seen at Selsdon on 10 July 1971 shortly after repaint and loss of its gold fleetname. *Gerald Mead*

Watch the Birdie

Below: The milkmaid of Romford smiles for the cameraman whose focus of attention is oily RML2262. *John May*

Lost in Kennington

Right: T1's predecessor, the B15 prototype Titan, is heading for Crystal Palace, not Charing Cross, on its southbound journey from Camden Town in October 1977. The destination blind on this vehicle had a habit of unrolling when the bus was in motion. *Steve Fennell*

3 CHARING CROSS
B15 Tomorrows Standards today
LEYLAND
TITAN
NHG 732P
FUNERAL SERVICE
MASONS
FUNERALS

Doom and Gloom

A dismal day, the dreary surroundings of Hertford bus station and battered RC10 combine to present a melancholy scene. The RC Green Line coaches were demoted to bus work in 1974 but survived only three more years. *John May*

Keeping Trim

Photographed in patchwork green at St Albans is SMW7, one of 15 Marshall-bodied Swifts acquired in 1971/2 from South Wales Transport. So far, the vehicle has kept its provincial embellishments but eventually these features were painted over or removed. *John May*

Tight Fit

The LT red bus map was just able to accommodate the southern terminus of Route 80 which, in this view at Burgh Heath, on 13 November 1975, was in the hands of RF338. Sutton garage lost its RF allocation for this service and the related Route 80A on 27 June 1976, two months after RF338 was withdrawn.
Michael Furnell

Fly Past

Left: Harrow Weald's RT2143 speeds along my old road, High Street, Harlington, on its way to Heathrow Airport, a few weeks before conversion of Route 140 to RM operation on 15 July 1978. RT2143 went on to enjoy an extended working life as a Chiswick Works skid bus and was one of only three RTs still in stock when LT ceased to exist on 29 June 1984. *Author*

Day Tripper

Right: Following LT's example, LCBS dabbled in all-over advertising, ex-Green Line coach RMC1480 being one of the victims. In this view taken on 4 May 1975, the Dartford-based vehicle has strayed off Route 401 and is entering Brighton. *Mike Harries*

INVICTA
co op
Hop on a bus
shop with us
And get a share of the profits
401
480 CLT

Factory Extension

Above: LS294 leaves old Kingston bus station on 7 September 1979 bound for the BAC works at historic Brooklands, a mile or so beyond the normal Route 219 terminus at Weybridge station. *Geoff Rixon*

Back Street Driver

Right: On its journey from North Finchley in April 1973, DMS575 is seen visiting the less salubrious areas of King's Cross. *Steve Fennell*

Friern Barnet
Wood Green
Finsbury Park
221
HOLBORN CIRCUS
Disney
THE Sun
Disney
THE Sun
PAY AS YOU ENTER
MLK575L

Out of the Blue

Left: A strange sight at Aldenham Works in the summer of 1972 was these two XFs which, together with XF7, had been painted in this striking livery (minus the red oxide patches!) for the Stevenage Blue Arrow services. Having operated there for nearly 2½ years, these buses would now revert to green livery and rejoin the remainder of the class at East Grinstead.
Steve Fennell

No Relief

Below left: Upholding NBC's corporate image has meant that there is little to distinguish LCBS's modernised RF48 from its Maidstone & District counterpart. In this view at Sevenoaks bus station on 29 October 1975, it is left to the pioneer Bristol LHS, BL1, to break the monotony of unrelieved leaf green. *Michael Furnell*

Night Shift

Right: RT837 passes through Streatham on Route N87 shortly before Brixton's RTs were replaced by DMs on 24 March 1975. The final scheduled RT-operated night services were Barking's routes N95 and N98 which lasted until 26/7 May 1978 when, in the face of increasing risks to crews, doored buses were introduced.
Steve Fennell

FOR SALE
£6
RED BUS PASS
Southcroft Road
Streatham Brixton
Kennington Road
Westminster Bridge
N87
CHARING CROSS
Take the Round London Sightseeing Tour
See more London with London Transport
BN 161
JXN 215

ODEON
202
HOUNSLOW
PAY AS YOU ENTER
PLEASE
MXX 488

Class Act in Richmond

Left: What a pleasure it is to feature a distinguished type, the AEC Regal IV, crossing an elegant Thames bridge! Sadly, this familiar scene would shortly disappear as Hounslow garage, the penultimate LT garage to operate RFs, replaced them on Routes 202 and 237 with BLs on 17 April 1977. *Mike Pope*

Commonplace

Below: Although outnumbered by the shorter Swifts, LCBS still had a sizeable fleet of Merlins: 109 out of the total of 665 built for LT between 1966-9. This country view of MB102 was taken on 22 August 1974 at Brockham Green, famous in the area for its Bonfire Night celebrations. *Michael Furnell*

Thin Green Line

Below: There is only a trace of traditional livery on RP7, one of three such coaches to carry all-over advertising in the early 1970s. The 90-strong RP class entered service from 18 December 1971 but, like so many contemporary vehicles, they suffered from reliability problems, with disposals starting in July 1979. This summer evening shot in Bell Street, Reigate, dates from July 1973. *Mike Harries*

Monarch of the Road

Right: Amidst the changing face of London over the centuries, King Charles I has remained seated on his horse, looking down Whitehall, since 1676. He will, of course, no longer be able to enjoy seeing members of the renowned RT family, represented here by RT2520 entering Trafalgar Square in 1973 on its journey from Raynes Park. *Mike Pope*

Euston Kingsway
Charing + Vauxhall
Clapham Junction
Wimbledon
77
KINGS CROSS
A fresh thought
from Danone.
DANONE
SINCLAIR
LONDON TRANSPORT

Slip of the Paintbrush

Left: RF495's claim to fame, in addition to being the chosen representative for the LT Museum collection, was having the wrong colours on the horizontal bar of the bull's-eye concealing the radiator cap. On 24 August 1978, the vehicle was caught on diversion passing Kingston Technical College. Seven months later, 27 years of RF operation at Kingston garage would come to an end. *Geoff Rixon*

Lighting-Up Time

Below left: The Bristol BN class was 6in narrower than the BLs but the difference would have been hard to discern but for the positioning of the side light/indicator unit assembly which was above, rather than alongside, the headlights. Leatherhead's BN38 passes through Wallington on a special Hospital Visitors' Service. *Dave Edwards*

Not for Sale

Right: The only Routemaster retained by LCBS after withdrawal was the fourth prototype, CRL4, seen here on the Welwyn Garden City Works service in its later guise of RMC4. Following retirement from Hatfield garage, this unique ECW-bodied Leyland coach was restored to its original LT Green Line livery for special duties. *Mike Pope*

Western Venturer
NATIONAL EXPRESS
LONDON COUNTRY

Southeast Suburban

DMS1685 passes the photographer's Morris Traveller (seen already in this book) as it climbs Bostall Hill, Plumstead on 10 November 1974. This was the first day of Fleetline operation on Route 99. *Michael Furnell*

Variety at Victoria

This interesting line-up consists of conventional RM683, unique FRM1 and ex-Bournemouth Transport DMO7. The latter was one of seven Fleetlines with removable roofs built in 1965 and purchased by LT in 1978. *Geoff Rixon*

Index of Locations Illustrated

Also of interest

abc London Buses
K. Lane ISBN: 0 7110 2596 7

abc London Transport Buses & Coaches 1948
S. Poole ISBN: 0 7110 2585 1

Bus Scene in Colour: Preserved Buses
P. Durham & G. Booth ISBN: 0 7110 2573 1

Glory Days: RT
K. McCormack ISBN: 0 7110 2581 9

Ian Allan Transport Library: AEC
A. Townsin ISBN: 0 7110 2620 3

Illustrated History of London's Buses
K. Lane ISBN: 0 7110 2516 9

London Trolleybus Chronology
M. Webber ISBN: 0 7110 2528 2

Routemasters in Colour
G. Rixon ISBN: 0 7110 2683 2

How to order: These books are available from most good bookshops or mail order by calling **Midland Counties Publications** on **01455 233747 (24 hour)** quoting the reference code **BA**, your credit card details (Visa/Mastercard/Switch/ Connect/Eurocard) and the ISBN(s) of the book(s) required. Alternatively, write to: **Midland Counties Publications, Unit 3 Maizefield, Hinckley Fields, Hinckley LE10 1YF. Fax: 01455 233737. E-mail:** midlandbooks@compuserve.com.
Post & packing charges: - UK customers please add 10% (minimum £1.50; maximum £3), orders over £40 are sent post-free. Overseas customers please add 15% (minimum £2), 10% for £150+ orders).

For further information on Ian Allan Publishing/OPC/Dial House titles visit our website at www.ianallanpub.co.uk.

Alternatively write to: **Ian Allan Publishing Ltd, Marketing Dept, Riverdene Business Park, Molesey Road, Hersham, Surrey KT12 4RG.**

Please include an A5 sae to the value of 50p. All titles available only while stocks last.